Free Lab

Design-build projects from the School of Architecture

Dalhousie University, Canada 1991-2006

Compiled and written by Christine Macy

Design by Youki Cropas

Tuns Press

Cover image: Chéticamp théâtre petit cercle, 2005.

© 2008 by the Faculty of Architecture and Planning
Dalhousie University
PO Box 1000, Central Station, B3J 2X4
Halifax, Nova Scotia, Canada

The work in this book has been carried out by the students and faculty
of the School of Architecture at Dalhousie University
Dean: Grant Wanzel
Director: Terrance Galvin

Project coordination, author and editor: Christine Macy
Design and layout: Youki Cropas
Secretarial support: Susanna Morash-Kent
Production assistance: Donald Westin, Tuns Press
Printing: Friesens

For more information on Tuns Press publications or Faculty programs,
please see the following websites: tunspress.dal.ca, archplan.dal.ca

Library and Archives Canada Cataloguing in Publication

Free lab : design-build projects from the School of Architecture, Dalhousie
University, Canada, 1991-2006 / Christine Macy.

ISBN 978-0-929112-56-5

1. Architecture--Nova Scotia--Halifax--21st century--Designs and plans.
2. Architecture, Modern – 21st century – Designs and plans. 3. Architectural
models--Nova Scotia--Halifax. 4. Dalhousie University. School of Architecture.
I. Title.

NA747.H29M32 2008   720.22   C2008-902967-4

Free Lab

C O N T E N T S

Foreword

*When I came here my priority – socially – was to fit in. Now I appreciate who I am –
I've not only learned architecture but I've also learned who I am. This is my calling,
my life. Most importantly, I am building a life for myself.*   Olly Chibua

For students, Free Lab is one of the most memorable moments in their architectural
education at Dalhousie University. Unlike most university education today, it is all about
hands-on learning – learning through doing. For architecture, that means designing and
creating real buildings and environments for people. While most studio design work is
for fictitious clients, with the skeletal program and schematic development appropriate to
learning lessons at certain stages of the educational process, Free Lab throws students into
the world of architecture with no holds barred. The result is an intense learning experience
for the students that takes them far beyond the classroom.

*It's the dilemma of our field [that] we spend a lot of time in the studio, imagining
buildings. To imagine and do at the same time is pretty rare.*   Ted Cavanagh

(Opposite page, from left to right and top to bottom)
Labyrinth 2005; Ripped Gridded Ribbon 2002; Schindler Frame 2002; Shambhala Outdoor Classroom 2003; Birchtown
Pavilion 1998; Gully Bridge 2002; Architecture in Motion 2 / Shadows 2004; Birchtown Benches 2002; Ghost.

The free labs were born of necessity – as an integrated learning experience during the sparsely staffed summer term – but they have grown into one of the most treasured experiences in the architectural programme. They are not required by any accreditation agency, university body, or graduate faculty. In fact, they serve no official function – but perhaps it is precisely this quality of being both completely supplementary and extra-curricular that makes the free lab so beloved by students and faculty. For true to their name, they offer a chance to learn, explore, and invent without preconceptions and judgment. Why is it that Free Lab participants always get high marks? Because everyone feels the effort has been total and the results extraordinary. Students shine in their area of expertise, bringing in skills no one knew they had and sometimes not even themselves.

Not surprisingly, labs have included all kinds of activities that architects find worthwhile – from travel labs to New York, London and Mexico City to labs that explore photography, video, drawing, collage, and digital fabrication. Students have created soundscapes, art installations, dance performances and drawing instruments. They have built studio partitions, participated in archaeological digs and created interpretive trails. They have designed stages and community gardens, saunas and sweat lodges, mobiles and stabiles, labyrinths, follies, sheds and buildings. But most free labs involve hands-on design and construction, and that is what students look forward to in the short and precious Canadian summer.

This book is a sampling of the over one hundred labs that have taken place in the school since 1991. The chapters are organized around themes that concern all building: site, culture, material, process and archetype. I have tried to show the variety and vitality of the free labs, while providing enough space for a more in-depth discussion of free labs that develop a body of work over several years. Generally, free labs are initiated by faculty who want to pursue an idea related to their research or practice. Some are responses to community groups who need help to realize a garden, an outbuilding, a trail, or other collective project. Some are developed by students who want to work with their classmates to realize a design of their own or one built for their parents, friends or first client. Sometimes a free lab is the first step a graduate student takes in developing his or her own research interest in architecture, an interest that will stay with them far into the future. Over the past ten years, many schools of architecture have begun to involve their students in design-build work like Free Lab, following the pioneering examples of Ball State University, Sam Mockbee, Steve Badanes, and Sergio Palleroni. Yet at Dalhousie University, we are fortunate to be able to make design-build an integral part of our architecture program that is available to all students. The design-build ethos of Free Lab can be felt throughout the school – in studio, technology, history, or theory courses alike.

Every summer, come the end of July, the people of Halifax look forward to the strange and fascinating constructions on the lawn of the architecture school, timed to coincide with the Atlantic Jazz Festival on the corner of Spring Garden Road and Queen Street. Then there's no doubt that the brick building with the columns in front isn't the courthouse or the public library. It is an architecture school, with students putting on a show for the entire city. And every year it's a different show. Of course, the labs on the lawn are a few of the many carried out each summer across the province and internationally. But wherever they happen, free labs demonstrate the value and importance of design as a concrete practice in real places, for the public.

In preparing this book, I'd like to thank the faculty, staff and students involved, for combing through their archives to contribute to this document, and to Dean Grant Wanzel and Tuns Press for enabling its publication.

Christine Macy

1 Landscape

Our book begins with landscape because all constructions start with a site. Nova Scotia is particularly blessed with extraordinary landscapes, especially maritime ones, because the province juts out into the Atlantic Ocean, enclosing the Bay of Fundy to its west and the Gulf of St. Lawrence to its north. The landscapes of Nova Scotia are in constant transformation, eroded by wind and water, deposited by prehistoric glacial drifts, and continually worked on by the daily actions of tides. The projects in this chapter explore the role of architecture in the landscape, and in so doing, they evoke the fragility of architecture in the face of geologic time. Resonating against their settings, they reveal layers of meaning and possibility that exist in the landscape but are often overlooked. They call on ideas of timelessness and eternity, of seasons and cycles, and they also bear witness to the transitory nature of human actions on the earth.

(Opposite page) Beach Wall 1997.
(Right) Glacial erratics and net at Peggy's Cove, 1998.

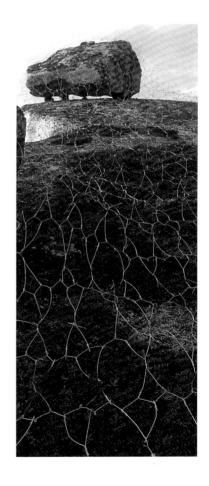

1.1 Beach Wall
Niall Savage, 1997

(Left to right) Detail of wood lath screen; Dune-swept fences offer a poetic setting for the wall; Sunset silhouette.
(Opposite page) A portal to the sea.

'Landscape' comes from *landskip*, the Dutch term for a painting of nature. This concept in turn was influenced by Italian landscape paintings, recreated by eighteenth century 'grand tourists' in gardens built on their return. These were called 'picturesque' gardens, because they resembled pictures of landscapes. The vision of landscape as a picture is one of the most enduring tropes of Western culture, and we see it here, in Beach Wall, in the form of a framing device erected on a deserted strand.

In this lab Savage was as interested in the material qualities of the screen that creates the wall as the 'picture window' it framed. Drawn to the rambling dune fences that retain sand and vegetation on the windswept spit of land, he echoed their repetitive slats and silhouetted framework to create a free-standing architectural screen that stands as a melancholy marker. As the province's coastal landscapes are gradually transformed from sites of labour to icons of natural beauty, such traces of human inhabitation recall former ways of life – one might think of the military ruins, lighthouse keeper's dwellings or shipwrecks that can be found on the rocky outposts of Nova Scotia's Atlantic shore.

1.2 Crystal Crescent Boardwalk

Catherine Venart, 2004

(Left to right) Woven wall delineates walkway to beach; Stone marker signals path to beach; Boardwalk seating with cairn.
(Opposite page) Site map; The boardwalk bench – a viewpoint to the shoreline and horizon.

In the Japanese landscape tradition, garden designers distinguish between landscapes for strolling in and landscapes for viewing. Some gardens have features of both, where one may sit and contemplate the garden scene, or stroll along a path and behold the garden gradually revealed. This interplay of perspective is explored in the next series of projects in this chapter.

Crystal Crescent beach consists of three interconnected beaches each with a distinct environment – from marsh ponds, to rock with low bush blueberries and evergreens, to white sand – linked by a boardwalk. Venart and her students documented the various layers and intersections of the three areas, developing a system of elements – including a ramp, boardwalk seating, sand dune fencing, and markers – that would reflect and define the specificities of the site. These elements were situated to emphasize and protect natural features and create linkages to the shore by marking beach entrances and viewpoints. Seating areas were developed to provide pause points along the boardwalk, to indicate beach access and contribute views of the shifting terrain of the shoreline.

This freelab explored landscape and threshold at Crystal Crescent Beach, on the Nova Scotian shore, close to the community of Sambro. We built on an existing walkway, linking three beaches with materials from the site, both natural and manmade. Catherine Venart

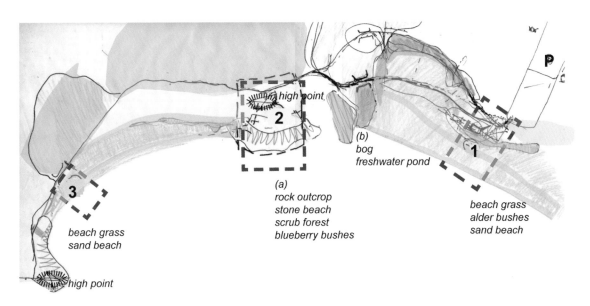

high point

2

(b)
bog
freshwater pond

P

1

(a)
rock outcrop
stone beach
scrub forest
blueberry bushes

beach grass
alder bushes
sand beach

3

beach grass
sand beach

high point

1.3   Exit 13A

Simon Ellison, Kevin Harrson, Michelle Johnson, Georgina Lyons, Ryan Mitchell, Geoff Moote, Matt Seegmiller, 2005   (Catherine Venart advising)

(Left to right) Undulations on the surface of the floating dock; Dock under construction; Distant view of the dock beached. (Opposite page) The dock in place at low tide; Looking out to sea at high tide.

Exit was a floating platform developed as an ever-shifting datum on the horizon manifesting the ebb and flow of the waterline between land and sky. The dock supports the viewer on softly undulating waves of wood, in turn supported by the ocean swells. The signature image is of the dock parallel to the horizon. It creates a second horizon, with 'waves' of wooden slats captured in frozen motion. That it is a site for reclining there is no doubt, since the gentle curve recalls Le Corbusier's famous reclining *chaise longue* of tile installed in the bath room of his Villa Savoie. In this way, the project doubles the gaze back on itself – it is both platform for viewing and a figure to be looked at.

1.4 Raftwerk
Roger Mullin, 2005

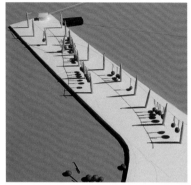  

(Left to right) Study model of possible configurations; Assembling the buoys; The installation site.
(Opposite page) Steps in the process.

This lab began with a brief for a site and program-specific installation on an abandoned pier in Halifax harbour. Working with flotation buoys, rope, re-bar and railway sleepers, students made a raft of these materials and floated it to the pier. They then disassembled the raft using the components to erect a long, surveyed line of buoys on site. The project celebrated found objects and sites and uncontrollable conditions, deriving its charge from the delicate balance between intention and circumstance. The project studied the prevalent phenomena of the edge between land and sea.

1.5 Hot Spot

Anke Wollbrink, 2006

(Left to right) Sheltering roof; View from sauna towards cold plunge; Roof extends over wood storage.
(Opposite page) Walkway at entrance to Hot Spot.

ART'insula is a residential seaside community on Nova Scotia's eastern shore near Sherbrooke. After designing a number of houses in the community, Wollbrink wanted to develop a more experimental project with Dalhousie architecture students. Struck by the typical wooden boardwalks that traverse the province's boggy beaches, she imagined one such boardwalk folded back on itself to form an enclosure where nature and architecture would meet. The purpose was to create a sauna and soaking pool that would be a lasting contribution to this community.

Working with local carpenters and engineers to refine their project, Wollbrink and the students worked on her design which created a strikingly simple form that simultaneously evokes groundscape, shed and chalet as it fits perfectly in the rock strewn heather. They were also delighted to find a fiberglass tank at a local fish farm which, when lined with boards and filled with pebbles at its base, formed an ideal cold plunge.

1.6 Salvation Army Urban Garden

Susan Molesky, 2006 - 2007

(Left to right) Garden site looking towards Gottingen Street; Construction in progress; Foundation for walls and benches. (Opposite page) The finished project.

A community garden built on the lot adjacent to the Salvation Army Booth Center for Men provides a space to socialize and enjoy the fresh air. The garden is divided into three spaces with a path stitching the site together. The 'porch' adjacent to the street is defined by a widened sidewalk, a concrete retaining wall, a planter and a cantilevered bench. A large granite stone found during the site excavations and a welded steel screen left to rust, evoking tall meadow grasses, create the threshold into the garden. The semi-public middle space is formed by two oval seating areas, one sunny with a raised bentwood cedar bench and round pavers, the other shady with a rock wall and grass. The back of the garden offers privacy. It is marked by a double-round brick barbeque. Most of the materials were donated or found on the site.

On any given day, the men are in the garden, enjoying the spaces; moving or changing the things within it (a giant sand lizard and a bird bath mysteriously appeared); and tending it. In addition to these informal activities, the Salvation Army has begun holding regular organized events in the garden.

1.7 Landscape Opera

Christine Macy, 1995

(Left to right) Boularderie Island meadow looking towards the Bras d'Or lakes; Beginning of the trail through the forest; Marking the threshold between land and water. (Opposite page) Installation at water's edge.

The final set of labs in this chapter are drawn to metaphysical, metaphorical or symbolic readings of the land to arrive at prehistoric – one might even say archetypal – interpretations of the earth and our place in it. These projects explore ritualistic inhabitation of the land.

The first of these, Landscape Opera, created archetypal spaces of inhabitation in field, forest and water's edge. The meadow site was a freshly scythed circle of grass. In the forest, a rope-wound tree uncoiled along a lantern-lit path to lead, Ariadne-like, through the dark forest to a bonfire. The seaside site was a rocky shore marked with menhirs and totems which students erected to mediate between rock and water. Such projects interpret the landscape to reveal how it might be inhabited, and explore the way the earth is reworked by natural and human forces alike. Macy sees architectural forms as fundamentally rooted in ritual practices. She asked students to describe an ancient ritual that might have taken place in these sites and from that, they developed their initial ideas for transforming each location.

1.8 Labyrinth

Timothy Collett and Patricia West, 2005

(Left to right) Building the labyrinth frame; Proceeding through the labyrinth; Aerial view.
(Opposite page, top to bottom) Labyrinth plan and elevations; Beach labyrinth.

The role of ritual in situating human activity on the land is as old as humankind, and Labyrinth explored how the primeval forms and geometries of the labyrinth could be applied to architecture. West and Collett began the laboratory with a one-day exercise constructing a classical labyrinth with stones on a nearby beach. The main installation was an adaptation of a medieval labyrinth plan. Designed to leave no trace, it was constructed by suspending a forest of coloured cardboard tubes from a high level grid of tensioned cables on the campus lawn. The density, size and colour intensity of the tubes were arranged in concentric rings to provide a changing experience and emphasize the rhythm of movement through the labyrinth. Suspended tubes guided the visitor and moved gently in the wind to create a beautiful object shimmering in the landscape.

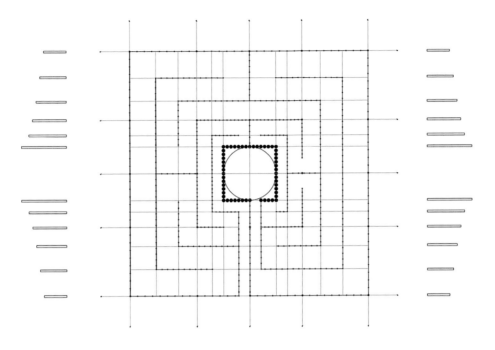

1.9 Erratic Net
Phillip Beesley, 1998

(Left to right) Expanding the groundscape; Extending skywards; A blanket on the horizon.
(Opposite page) Inside the erratic net.

The final lab in this chapter took the operation of geological time as inspiration for an installation that tries to quite literally inhabit the earth. The delicate expanded mesh of Erratic Net aimed to create a liminal space of inhabitation out of the expanded earth.

> *The textile is organized into alternating peaks and valleys, presenting barbs outward catching new material and inward for anchoring beneath. These anchors hold the net just above the bare rock, making a shallow film of still, sheltered air allowing delicate growth to emerge. The net is made with wire joints clamped by sliding flexible tubes that lock each link to its neighbour making a tough, resilient structure. Such large-scale field structures offer immersion, an expansion rendering our physical bodies porous and offering wide-flung dispersal of identity.*
> Philip Beesley

For Beesley, to immerse oneself into the larger field is to lose one's sense of separateness – it is a union, verging on the ecstatic, that is situated in the mystical tradition.

This project can be understood as an extension of the ordinary industrial practice of reinforcing landscapes using geotextiles, while it relies heavily on an emotional response in people who encounter the work. It explores individual boundaries, both psychological and physical. Philip Beesley

2 Culture

Each landscape in Nova Scotia has made its distinctive mark on the people who live there. The province is as rich in cultural landscapes as it is natural ones – from the earliest inhabitants whose descendents still populate the province, to successive wave of immigrants and settlers, and the current generations of people who call Nova Scotia their home, if only for the years they are studying here. While free labs may begin with a request from a community group, they often develop into a long-term commitment that allows students and faculty to return year after year to build in a certain place. This kind of exchange is about building culture: in the students, between the university and local communities, in artifacts and landscapes. The connection to community may be what makes the free lab so important.

(Opposite page) Eskasoni Studio under construction, 2002.
(Right) Erecting the scaffolding for the Story Arch 1995.

2.1 Birchbark Canoe

Richard Kroeker, 1991

(Left to right) Canoe components; Shaping and tensioning the birchbark to form the canoe.
(Opposite page) Project story-line.

The birchbark canoe is a wonderful starting point to talk about the role of culture in design. One of the oldest designs in North America, it remains also one of the most sophisticated crafts – along with the kayak – to be found anywhere. This two week lab took students through the process of making a canoe, with each step in the fabrication process forming the template for a subsequent step.

> *The birchbark canoe is lightweight, structurally strong, dynamic, and culturally expressive – all those things we try to achieve with any good design. It could be easily broken down into components for repair or trade. It was an accessible technology which allowed for relatively easy travel across a continent through all kinds of waters, using materials from the landscape connected through a brilliantly conceived set of details. In that sense it is the quintessential expression of this landscape and our shared cultures in this place.* Richard Kroeker

2.2 Mi'kmaq Lodges

Richard Kroeker, John Henry Lafford, Albert Marshall and Barry Bernard, 1994

(Left to right) Selecting birch saplings; Forming the domes; Thatched lodges.
(Opposite page) A traditional Mi'kmaq sweat lodge under construction.

These traditional sweat lodges were built with the assistance of John Henry Lafford and Barry Bernard. Birch saplings anchored at the edges of the building are interwoven horizontally to form a dome, which is then thatched with balsam branches. The oil in the balsam sheds water, breathes, and has a scent that repels black flies.

> *In learning how to make these traditional shelters, we realized the nestedness of culture in the greater natural world – we were merely re-arranging materials that are already there. One thing I learned from John is that everything in the forest has useful information – one just has to open one's eyes. All nature is full of information. What we bring as designers is our mind: the ability to read that information, and values according to which we organize that information. Architecture, in this sense, results from site and mind.*   Richard Kroeker

Building is not a thing to be repeated. Each time one builds, one must apply the mind to the process. The finished building then has layers and layers of information. For example, one symbol of the Mi'kmaq nation is the star shape. Building these lodges, we noticed this symbol imbedded in the reflected ceiling plan of the structure, in the reality of building. Richard Kroeker

2.3 Eskasoni Studio and Conference Room
Richard Kroeker for Murdena Marshall, 2001-2003

(Left to right) Structural frame of spruce timber trusses (2001); Diagonal strapping and insulation (2002); Completed studio with its shingle roof (2006). (Opposite page, from left) Studio interior; Night time view during construction.

Much of what is built in Canada uses wood from the forest and is built within the forest, or what was once the forest. Many of the processes by which we use the forest for building seem to be approaching obsolescence. This project...questions the ways in which our assumptions about technology have conditioned the current thinking on how wood is used in building.   Richard Kroeker

Kroeker's work has explored the architectural potentials for small-dimensioned timber, a regional resource that is commercially used for paper pulp rather than building material. Drawing from ten years of work in this area, Kroeker included students in the design and construction process of a studio and meeting room in the Mi'kmaq community of Eskasoni, an extension to the home of elder and educator Murdena Marshall. The structural frame is made of freshly harvested black spruce trees, bent into arched forms and bound with other timbers to create trusses. Pinned at the ridge and base, they form a series of frames that are sheathed with diagonal cladding, insulated and shingled on the exterior. The result has the clarity and grandeur of an Algonquian longhouse, yet is a modern, tightly insulated building.

This building is a reflection of who we are as Mi'kmaq people. The actual project is the window of our past in which it fosters the need for us people to ensure that the environment will be there for the future generations. Our objective is to leave the world in a better place that we are currently using. There is no need for us to compromise the future generations' opportunities of sustaining themselves.

Albert and Murdena Marshall

2.4 Birchtown Pavilion

Richard Kroeker, 1998

(Left to right) A new roof for the 'pit house'; An analogous pavilion in Halifax; Night view, showing thatched roof and rock-filled wooden crib foundations. (Opposite page) Completed pavilion on the school lawn.

Free Labs occasionally grow out of design studios and studios develop out of free labs. This lab began in May of 1998 when Kroeker led a speculative reconstruction of the kind of 'pit dwelling' that housed the early Black Loyalists in the first fierce winters of 1789 when they settled on the rocky shores of Nova Scotia. Using an archaeologically-excavated ruin of such a pit dwelling as their foundation, Kroeker's students erected a framework of local spruce timbers, lashing them together with flexible spruce root and cladding the roof with marsh grass and balsam boughs.

The one-day exercise was developed further as a July free lab back at the school, when students reworked the techniques they had learned to create a modern pavilion on the school lawn in time for the annual Jazz Festival.

2.5 Birchtown Benches & Interpretive Trail
Christine Macy, 2002 and 2004

(Left to right) Laying stone foundations; Mixing mortar; Thatch cladding on historic reconstruction of 'pit dwelling'.
(Opposite page) Students assemble outside the Birchtown church on the historic site.

The Black Loyalist community of Birchtown in southwestern corner of the province has hosted numerous studios and free labs in and around the evocative ruins of the earliest Black settlers and the living landscape of their descendants. These two labs contributed to the creation of an interpretive trail through the woods near the archaeological digs and historic buildings of the settlement.

In the first lab, student built benches and interpretive viewpoints in a rustic 'park architecture' style, and in the second one they developed cladding for an archaeologically reconstructed pit-house, using spruce boughs and thatched marsh grass. With interpretive assistance from Ken Brown of the Black Loyalist Heritage Society and curatorial help from David Carter of the Nova Scotia Museum, they also designed and installed panels interpreting the immediate cultural landscape of an eighteenth century quarry and the ruins and traces of a bygone era.

2.6   Mexico City: Three Eras of the Zocalo
Sarah Bonnemaison and Christine Macy, 1999

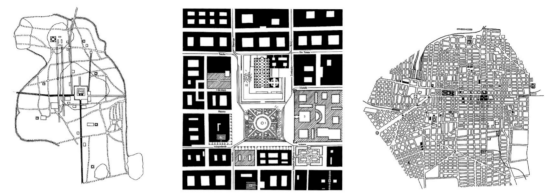

(Left to right) The canal city of Tenochtitlan during Aztec rule (1519); Mexico City's *Zocalo* in 1900; The modernizing city (1920-35). (Opposite page) A day at the market in the ceremonial centre of Aztec Mexico, adapted from Marquina Solomon Gonzalez-Blanco Garrido, *The Great Temple of Mexico* (1993).

This lab brought ten students to Mexico City in a month-long study of its central square, known as the Zocalo. Drawing from Macy and Bonnemaison's long-standing interest in festival architecture, students were asked to study the plaza across history, looking equally at its physical characteristics and the activities it supported as Aztec Tenochtitlan, the Baroque capital of New Spain, and the modern-day centre of an independent Mexico. Working in civic and federal archives, students unearthed original maps and drawings that revealed the incredible richness of cultural life in the different epochs – and testifying to Aldo Rossi's idea that architectural forms persist in the midst of constant change.

The Zocalo was revealed as marketplace and temple under Aztec rule, supplied by canals with the riches of empire; as the seat of colonial power under the fierce Catholicism of the Spanish colonizers; and as the symbolic locus of an independent mestizo culture in the heady days of independence. Field trips to Teotihuacan, the baroque cities of Puebla and Oaxaca, and the modernist works of Luis Barragan complemented the lab.

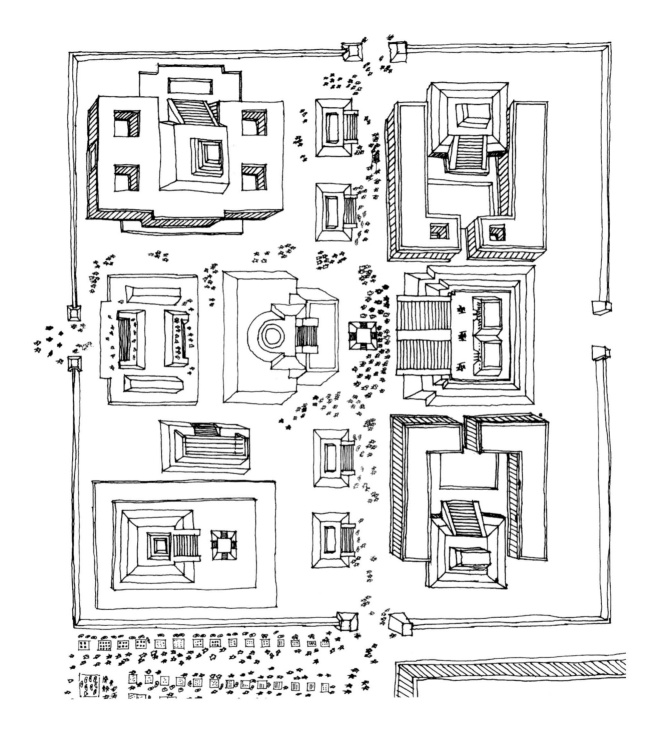

2.7 Shambhala Outdoor Classroom & Saint Joseph's Daycare Playground
Kim Thompson, 2003 and 2004

(Left to right) Making cob with the "foot dance"; Applying cob by hand; Surface detail of a lion gargoyle in cob.
(Opposite page) Freelab group with their tools on the site.

This first of these labs involved building an outdoor classroom on an empty asphalt lot adjacent to the Shambhala School in Halifax. The school wanted to extend the learning environment to the outdoors in a space that would evoke imagination. Working with youth from the school, Dalhousie architecture students formed the walls of the outdoor classroom with cob, an adobe-like material made of clay, straw, sand and water. The result was a small amphitheatre and a sitting area formed around the spine of a dragon.

> *It's interesting they would choose a dragon because only later did they find out that creature is a prominent symbol in Shambhala iconography. In the Shambhala community the energy of the dragon is [...] said to encourage openness, exertion and delight – exactly the qualities the school wants to foster in the children who will use the space.* Steve Mustain, director of Shambhala School

It was an amazing experience. I felt like I was sharing something of my culture with the people of Halifax. It felt very connected for me. At home people are trying so hard to get away from materials like mud to become more western. Here I was building a classroom out of the very material some people at home shunned. Olly Chibua, student

2.8 Story Arch

Christine Macy, 1995

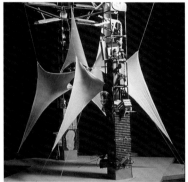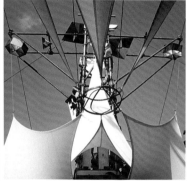

(Left to right) Scale model in the studio; Looking up through the 'dream catcher'; Storytelling and music under the arch. (Opposite page) The ephemeral installation in front of the School of Architecture during the summit week.

In 1995 Halifax was the site for a G7 Summit, when leaders of industrialized countries from Europe and North America convene to discuss shared political interests. This lab involved the construction of a temporary arch, much like the ones built for royal entries in the major cities of Europe and the colonial towns of the British Empire. This arch however was not designed to show fealty to the ruling elite, but to tell the stories of local peoples and communities which often are not heard. Students developed sculptural compositions representing many of these communities in Nova Scotia – cultural groups, such as the Mi'kmaq, Acadians and Afro-Nova Scotians; and communities of experience or interest, such as coal miners, fishermen, inventors, and the like. When these allegorical sculptures were assembled in the cells of two large scaffolding towers, they supported a delicate tensile roof between them. The municipal library held storytelling sessions beneath the arch throughout the summit week.

The lab included students from a Grade Seven class from Rockingham School, giving a younger generation a feeling for design at work.

Canada's tradition of welcoming arches built for dignitaries, dating from the nineteenth century, was descended from a practice common in the Renaissance and even Ancient Rome. These often marvellous architectural ephemera have left few traces. Yet, such architecture was an important reservoir of collective memory for subjects, and later, citizens. Some of Canada's early arches were built by people in industries (lumber, fishing or mining) and cultural groups (Chinese, Japanese), to express their support for British rule. This lab turned that tradition on its head to bring to light Nova Scotian stories during an event characteristic of an increasingly global and impersonal world. Christine Macy

2.9 Chéticamp théâtre petit cercle

Ted Cavanagh, Richard Kroeker, Roger Mullin and Alden Neufeld, 2004

Collaborative Practice Award, ACSA, 2005; Gold Medal, National Post Design Exchange, 2005;
Lt. Governor's Masterwork Award, sponsored by ScotiaBank, 2006

(Left to right) A windbreak in the landscape; Looking into the theatre; Playground fixtures brought into the design.
(Opposite page) The construction process.

In 2004, Acadian communities across the maritime provinces celebrated 400 years of European settlement in Canada by hosting the Third Worldwide Acadian Congress. In the town of Cheticamp on Cape Breton island, organizers planned temporary festival sites and talked optimistically about establishing a permanent summer theatre camp in their community. In this context, two dozen architecture students and three professors went to work to build a 180 seat children's amphitheatre on a derelict school playground, made of lumber and salvaged materials in a two-week building event that generated genuine excitement in the community.

The theatre is made of one-by-three slats over a frame of vertical ribs ballasted with rocks, creating a wind-sheltered zone for the audience. Salvaged bleachers adapted to the lens-shaped space brought the audience close to the stage. The success of the project as an example of community-based architecture has led to several prizes, and $300,000 in further funding to complete the theatre camp. It is dedicated to the memory of architecture student Colin Gash.

2.10 Chéticamp Sleeping Cabins

Ted Cavanagh, Roger Mullin and Peter Sassenroth, 2006

(Left to right) Assembling the first 'wheel'; All parts are laid out and ready for mounting; The 'keystone' completes the structure. (Opposite page) Lightweight fins and a plywood skin form the interchangeable wedges for a wheel; Colourful wiffle balls offset the tensile roof for ventilation.

The free lab returned to Chéticamp two years later, with a request to create sleeping cabins for children participating in the summer theatre camps. But because the cabins were to be set up in the school courtyard, they had to be completely demountable for storage during the winter months. The solution was a modular system made of plywood to support four bunk beds and a small deck within a circular cross section that has the playful feel of a toy airplane fuselage or submarine.

> *The thing that's really strong about it is that the whole community was involved. Once they saw what we were doing, everybody wanted to help in every way they could.* Ted Cavanagh

3   Material

The best architecture shows an appreciation for what materials can do and what can be done with them. It is a dialogue that is best experienced first-hand as students encounter building materials in all of their wonderful capability and intransigence. Much of the poetry of architecture comes from one material meeting another across the joint or 'the detail'. According to eighteenth century German architectural theorists, much of architecture's rhetorical power lay in this moment of joinery they called 'tectonics', or the artistry of assembly – and modern architecture continues to privilege the detail.

This next set of free labs explores the characteristics of materials in design – taking them as found in nature and modifying them through artifice, or finding them in the surplus of our consumer society. All of the labs eschew mass-produced standardized building materials and demand invention and ingenuity in the design process.

(Opposite page) Finding Form in natural materials 2003.
(Right) Re-using and recycling, Wooden Monkey 2004.

3.1 Grid Shell

Richard Kroeker and John Henry Lafford, 1995

(Left to right) Laying out the grid and binding the connections; Hoisting the vault in place; Completing the frame.
(Opposite page) Grid shells on Boularderie Island, Cape Breton.

The grid shell structures on Boularderie Island were made of birch saplings bent into a lattice shell structure. The goal was to explore the long span capability of that material, which in the structure above turned out to be a twenty-foot span that held the weight of two students on top.

> *John Lafford knows his material and structure, and he felt this structure had terrible connections. We had cut the saplings and tried to wire the blunt ends together. Now we are leaving the branches on the tree, and weaving branch ends to branch ends. John suggested we split the remaining butt ends into quarters or sixths and weave those together. Now we can span farther, by using the first layer as an armature and adding saplings as required.* Richard Kroeker

3.2 Ripped Gridded Ribbon
Peter Sassenroth, 2002

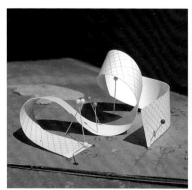  

(Left to right) Study model of the 'ribbon'; Assembling the lath strips into a grid framework; Moving the ribbon to the site. (Opposite) Forming the curve and fastening the layers of lath; The finished structure.

In this lab, Sassenroth explored the expressive potential of continuous curvature in a ribbon-like pavilion on the front lawn of the school. Working with scrap wood, students assembled long strips of lath into a lattice, and positioned the resulting 'ribbon' into a number of curved configurations, stabilizing it by connecting the four layers of lath to one load-bearing profile and forming a grid-shell-like structure. The exercise was a first-hand exploration in form-finding in the spirit of Frei Otto's Institute for Lightweight Structures.

3.3 Gully Bridge and Finding Form
Roger Mullin, 2002 and 2003

(Left to right) Gully Bridge: Using jigs to bend the green wood trusses; Measuring the span; Setting the primary members in place. (Opposite page) Finding Form: a bent wood tower on the front lawn.

These two labs explore the potentials of bent wood in structural framing. The first lab built a pedestrian bridge across a small ravine on a First Nations reserve in Prince Edward Island. Students felled black spruce trees and formed the still green timbers into curved trusses.

The following year, similar trusses erected vertically in the ground created a directional field of stiffened columns within a skeletal framework – a rustic gothic. Within this framework, dimensional lumber was woven basket-like, its lengths overlapped to form the asymmetrically curved enclosure. The result is completely novel – a tower with characteristics both familiar and strange. As a former student, Mullin is the second generation of designer to pursue this way of working at the school and as such, one can see his work as a kind of 'deconstruction' and re-thinking of green wood construction.

3.4 Summer Kitchen

Kim Thompson and Jean d'Aragon, 1996

(Left to right) Outdoor oven in the summer kitchen; Peephole; Kitchen and house. (Opposite page) Tamping down the roof.

For ten years, Thompson's free labs have introduced Dalhousie students to natural building materials and systems – including cob, earth and lime plasters, straw bale, wattle and daub, low impact foundations, and living roofs. This lab was one of her earliest efforts, carried out in collaboration with a post-professional M.Arch. student Jean d'Aragon who, like Thompson, has focused his design work exclusively on such natural building systems. Students relish the opportunity to explore the sculptural qualities of earth construction in their finish work. Design and hands-on work are focused on a client or community group that eagerly anticipates the completed project.

3.5 Playful Walls Ship Harbour Studio
Kim Thompson, 2005

(Left to right) Proud participants in front of the studio; Feels good on the hands; Tying bales together.
(Opposite page) Measuring and scribing before the next piece is set into place.

This small studio was a site for experiments in earth construction during an intensive building session. The frame and roof were finished before the lab began, allowing students to focus their energies on wall systems such as cob and wood, plastered straw bales, and wattle and daub. A living roof produced a harvest of acorn squash that fall. This lab also asked students to visit five earlier projects to understand what, in natural building materials, works best in the demanding Canadian maritime climate.

We are constructing totems and talisman – reminders of best practices and an inspiring repertoire of what is possible when communities build together. Kim Thompson

3.6 Wooden Monkey

Tyler Dixon, Kelly Dodman, Gabe Prost, Sony Rai, Yiming Wang, Barry Wong, 2004
(Steven Mannell advising)

(Left to right) Laced recliner; Collage coffee table; Detail of woven ribbon settee. (Opposite page) Tea, anyone?

The next four labs work with salvaged materials, satisfying an ethical as well as a practical ambition – to be thrifty with material and to transform one person's waste into another's delight through the wonderful alchemy of good design. Wooden Monkey was a student-led effort to provide outdoor furniture for the restaurant of the same name on Halifax's summer promenade of Argyle Street. Their free-spirited and playful juxtaposition of materials communicated exactly the kind of creative and original image desired by the owners of this alternative vegetarian restaurant.

3.7 Ambient Material
Phonebook Building in a Recycling Depot
Richard Kroeker, 2005

(Left to right) Woven wood cladding; Material studies; Phonebook beams and "masonry" walls.
(Opposite page) The pavilion shows that one person's waste is another person's resource.

In this free lab, students used everyday materials found in the natural or industrial environment to create a building system – some examples given were sand, newspaper, cable, trees, wooden pallets, tires, car doors, stone, phone books, or recycled windows. The process required them to work out details for a prototype structure, such as walls, beams, arches, connections or foundations. The details could be prefabricated in the school or built on site.

> *The free lab asks students to learn from materials and explore how they behave. We decided on a set of experiments to test what these materials could do. Everyone did experiments – they then had to exchange the models and work on someone else's model to refine the idea. Rather than agree on what it would look like (the form), we agreed on a process, making decisions on the site. Eventually, students begin to see that external form results from a way of working.*
> Richard Kroeker

3.8 Greenhouse
Ilona Hay, 2005

(Left to right) Pattern of walls and screens; Water-filled bottles in their framework; The structure is nearly complete.
(Opposite page) Ready to receive the seedlings.

Starting with the simple question of what plants require in a greenhouse, Hay led students through an exploration of the microcosm of a growing environment. First, they decided their brief was to extend the growing season for tomatoes and basil by two to four months. Investigations of solar exposure, humidity, envelope, and ventilation led to discussions of ecology and sustainability, which resulted in a student decision to use recycled materials as much as possible. Recycled bottles filled with water were assembled into structural bays. After heating up all day, these would release stored heat at night for the plants. A rich harvest of post-election endorsement signs were incorporated into the cladding, and grocery bags were used as pots for the plants.

After finding their client – a community garden association – students adapted the design to accommodate nearby garden plots while still facing the sun. Adding a trellis for a grapevine, they left the community gardeners with a lovingly assembled and restrained architectural bricolage, carefully detailed to create a sophisticated structure out of a work-a-day garden building.

3.9   LIGHTsail

Timothy Gray, 2006

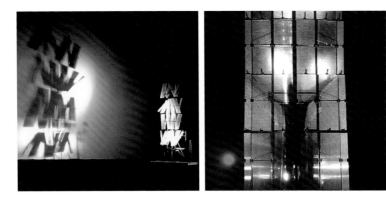

(Left to right) Play of light; The wizard manages the effects; Light sail by day next to the grain elevator.
(Opposite page) Projecting light and capturing it (on camera).

This lab takes as its departure point the Halifax grain elevators, an urban monument that overwhelms the small wooden houses it adjoins. Struck by the contrasts in this site, Gray proposed a device that would in a sense 'bridge' the abyss of scale, allowing human actions to make their mark on the massive wall of the elevators. The result was the Lightsail, a site-specific installation reminiscent of Lazlo Moholy-Nagy's light modulators, which screen and manipulate light to form playful and evocative shadows.

Scouring a nearby warehouse for materials, students found a number of diffusers from everyday fluorescent light fixtures, and they transformed these into the central elements of the project. Mounted on a steel mast so they could rotate and pivot freely, the diffusers created a mechanical veil for the projected light. Activated by a breeze or by a person, the Lightsail projects a play of shadow combining both geometric and human silhouettes onto the silo walls.

4 Process

'Building' is a verb as well as a noun, and every architect knows that to make a good building is a long process that involves many steps and many participants along the way. These labs focus on the design process, taking students on an adventure of discovery – one that reveals design less as *parti* and more as a methodical and layered work. Some of these labs involve multiple stages of work like a scientific experiment, where suppositions are developed and tested. Others establish a field of action for student invention. Still others set up a pedagogical framework where each step a student makes takes them to a position where they can make the next one. Design development is the lesson here.

(Opposite page) Constructing a minimal surface, Tensile Pattern 1997.
(Right) Study model by Kevin Reid, From Drawing to Building 2002.

4.1 Tensile Pattern
Sarah Bonnemaison, 1997

(Left to right) Birds-eye view; Prototype tents provide a little shade in the July heat; Shack-form and tent-form.
(Opposite page) The finished tent pitched at Martin's Point on Mahone Bay.

To create architectural surfaces from fabric, designers employ techniques from the textile arts – for most architects, one of the most challenging aspects of this work is to think not in terms of orthogonal geometries, but in terms of complex curves created from flat materials. The missing link is the pattern. This lab took students through a step-by-step process of making patterns without the aid of computers. First, they learned how to deconstruct a three dimensional shape into a two dimensional surface, by creating a pattern for a familiar object like a fruit. They then designed and modeled a tensile structure that used double curvatures, and finished the lab by collaborating to realize two of the twelve designs at full scale, the one shown here designed by Andy Moy.

4.2 Mov-ibles

Marie-Paule Macdonald, 2000

(Left to right) Making it 'fit'; Swinging bench-door; Folding, sliding and hinged panels.
(Opposite page) Mov-ible folly on the front lawn.

Many free labs call on the venerable tradition of the architectural folly. This is a work of architecture with no purpose other than its own architectural idea. In the eighteenth century, follies were often garden pavilions laden with evocative historical or symbolic meanings – from eroticism to freemasonry. In the late twentieth century, Hans Peter Wörndl and other architects created follies to explore architecture's rhetorical potentials. Freed from purpose, a folly can sometime unleash the most surprising possibilities and new experiences.

In this lab, Macdonald, a professor of architecture at Waterloo, returned to her native province to have some fun on the front lawn of the school. Here, nothing is what it seems, as a wall opens up to be a door and reveals a room hidden inside, roofs become doors, and doors fold out to form benches.

4.3 From Drawing to Building

Anthony Viscardi, 2002

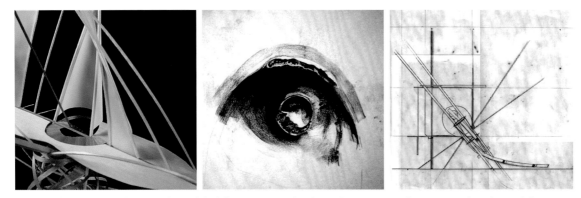

(Above left) Amelia Hollingsworth: model. (Above centre and right, and opposite page) Craig Brimley: charcoal drawings of a cast, maquette elevation and cast maquette supported by structural framework.

In a departure from most free labs, this project took students on a step-by-step process of creating complex forms and spaces from a simple beginning. A summer visitor from Lehigh University in Pennsylvania, Viscardi asked students to make a cast of a found object. When the cast was opened up, the negative of the mold contained new and unexpected forms. Ruled drawings of these revealed lines of tension and organization, which in turn suggested skeletal armatures and further spatial developments. The scaffolding could, of course, then be employed to support the original cast. The lab left a trail of exquisite drawings and models in various media that astonished everyone, not the least the students at what they had accomplished.

> *In this process of investigation and discovery, drawings are a scaffolding; a temporary architecture that leaves its trace in the final construction, allowing 2-D and 3-D to collude in the process of design. Discovery is short-circuited when design is too goal oriented. When design becomes more investigative and analogical, students open up to unstereotypical thinking and to amazement.*
> Anthony Viscardi

Anthony Viscardi's free lab was amazing, he challenged us every step of the way which allowed us to create structures beyond our imagination, he believed that these were from our subconscious. He had a rigorous production schedule, 10:00 am lecture 10:00 pm pin up! Robert Osbourne, student

4.4 Fixing the Light

Kourosh Mahvash, 2003

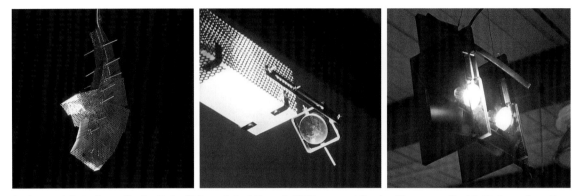

(Left to right) Light studies by Farhad Mawani, Earl Peng, Jeff Skinner and Sandra Thompson; Sophia Dobrev, Greg Fry and Alex Kravec; Danielle Churchill, J.P. Felix and Michelle McDonough. (Opposite page) Light fixture by Tim Schmitt.

This free lab was an opportunity for students to apply architectural skills to the field of industrial design. Inspired by his own interest in light, Mahvash asked students to develop a new light fixture for the school's exhibition room, one that would meet the exhibition lighting specifications of the Illuminating Engineering Society of North America. The lab comprised five stages: case study, contextual study, conceptual design, specification and fabrication. Working in groups and on their own, students designed, built and installed light fixtures that were judged by faculty and students at the end of the lab. The winning design was by Tim Schmitt.

4.5 Architecture in Motion 1 / Traces

Sarah Bonnemaison and Christine Macy, with Sondra Loring and Jill-Ann Schwartz, 2003

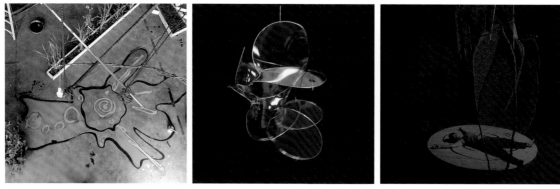

(Left to right) Trace of the dancer's movement in plan; Movement model; Performance night.
(Opposite page) Afternoon before opening night.

This workshop brought architecture students together with choreographers and dancers to create an installation and dance performance in a former industrial warehouse in Hudson, New York. In a low-tech version of the motion tracing techniques developed by ergonomic scientists in the early twentieth century, students traced dancers' movements in sand. When the sand was swept away and the drawings traced in charcoal, students had a 'reference plan' on the ground. They then used wire to model the movement in space and dipped these models in a soap film to find minimal surfaces. The resulting full-scale environments, directly derived from dancers' choreographies, formed set pieces for the dancers to re-interpret their movement phrases for the final piece, performed in front of a packed audience the last evening of the lab.

> *It was not just about dance – it was about understanding the space around us and interpreting that space. It gets you involved with people from different professions, working together towards a common goal. Being able to work with non-architects opens your eyes to new ideas.... To present our final performance for 100 people from Hudson, New York, was unbelievable. How often do architects have a chance to do something like that?* Lefoko Simako, student

As a dancer, I had already imagined the architecture of dance – the structure of the body and the possibilities of the blank space of the stage. But, as I realized on the first day of Traces, I had never thought about the dance of architecture – the movement within inanimate forms, how those same concepts that describe kinetic motion can also describe seemingly static structures. Tatiana Margitic, dancer

4.6 Architecture in Motion 2 / Shadows

Sarah Bonnemaison, Christine Macy and Kourosh Mahvash, with Sondra Loring, Ariella Pahlke and Jill-Ann Schwartz, 2004

(Left to right) Dancer Maria Osende walks through the 'grass'; Speeds of motion; Laban movement choir beneath mobile.
(Opposite) Multiplying space and movement with a video capturing its own projection.

The following year, the architecture and motion free lab took on two dozen students, again in collaboration with Sondra Loring and her company of dancers. This time, the challenge was to transform a generic 'white box' theatre into a vivid world of space, light and colour. As in the previous year, students were again brought into the performance as the *corps de ballet* – which required weeks of rigorous physical exercises led by dancers to discover the spatial implications of their bodies as individuals and as a group. They also explored the relationship between architectural statics and body mechanics, between body displacements in space and geometries found in architectural plans. The sets became large mobiles, formed from organic and industrial materials from local farms and recycling centres, which served as interactive set pieces for the dancers and instruments for shadow projection. With the assistance of a professional video artist, students were able to multiply the visual effects, creating a kaleidoscope of form and motion that was unforgettable.

4.7   Architecture in Motion 3 / Gestures
Sarah Bonnemaison and Christine Macy, with Joel Dauncey, Maria Osende and Ariella Pahlke 2005

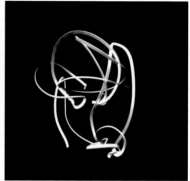

(Left to right) Maria Osende develops movement phrase; Motion caption trails in Maya software; Stereotomic model of motion capture. (Opposite page) Completed structure in courtyard of the Maritime Museum.

The third architecture and motion lab involved an installation in the courtyard of Halifax's Maritime Museum. Before the lab began, the research group of architects, videographer and dancer had recorded everyday life on the waterfront, interpreted these through choreographed sequences, and recorded them on a motion capture stage to create three dimensional 'traces' of the movement. Working with Maya animation software, digital and stereolithographic plaster models, and ultimately wooden models to predict the behavior of the building materials, the team developed the basic forms of the pavilions.

During the two week free lab, students developed construction details using boat-building techniques of wood steaming, bending, glue-laminating, planing, sanding, riveting, finishing, and joinery; concrete forming for the footings; and tensile pattern-making, colour-mixing, and hand-dying for the netting. And inevitably, they were an irresistible exhibit of craftsmanship at work for the many curious visitors impressed by their industry and skill. The pavilions remained in place for three years.

5 Archetype

The closing chapter of our book on free labs presents a number of projects that look to the past for inspiration and for lessons in the first principles of design. Architecture by architects has its roots in the Italian Renaissance, and we need only think of Brunelleschi's device for picturing his project in the cathedral plaza of Florence to see that optics is centrally important to architectural effect. The first two labs in this chapter address the perception of architectural space – the fundamental relation, one might say, of architecture as a visual art.

The next set of labs looks at the building lessons that can be discovered in past works and which, through reconstructions of these projects, students can learn first hand. Lastly, we close with a number of projects that draw from the timeless qualities of vernacular structures in Nova Scotia to create highly abstracted works of modern architecture that themselves suggest a timeless or archetypal quality.

(Opposite page) Zumthor Chapel, 2003.
(Right) Ghost 3 in Kingsburg, Nova Scotia, 1997.

5.1 Camera Obscura
Ken Kam, 2003

(Left to right) Ready; Set; Action!
(Opposite) Capturing a stiller and quieter perspective of the world.

Camera, the Latin word for 'room', is known to us today as the name of a device that captures images on film. Yet in the sixteenth century, artists commonly used a device that was both room and viewing apparatus. The marvellous quality of a camera obscura (literally, dark room) is to turn the world into a picture – a silent moving picture that one can see in great detail without being seen. In this free lab, Kam asked students to build a working camera obscura, and then to use it in various locations around town, to record on light-sensitive paper the images obtained. The results are a reminder that vision is very personal and inevitably determined by the instruments being used.

5.2 Architects of Illusion: Perceptions of Deceptions

Eric Van Duzer and Leslie Van Duzer, 2006

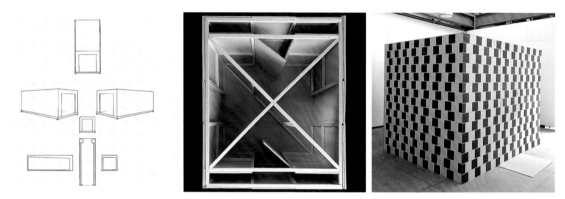

(Left to right) An exercise in hiding space; Model of the illusionistic room from above; Optical illusions on the outside. (Opposite page, top to bottom) Mirrors make it difficult to see what's really there; Lab participants magically appear.

The result of a collaboration from the brother-sister team of education professor and illusion artist Eric Van Duzer and architecture professor Leslie Van Duzer, this lab introduced students to the art of designing spatial illusions. After a grounding on the seven principal ways space can be made to seem larger or smaller than it is, students were asked to practice their skills in designing the equipment behind such illusions by hiding a shoe in a box seemingly far too small to accommodate it.

The group soon progressed to the design of a room – open on two sides with doors (and mirrors, of course) that expanded and multiplied the space. But not even meticulous study could account for the way seven participants in the lab appeared from a seemingly empty room! The illusionistic theme wrapped the outside of the room with the Café Wall Illusion that danced around the surface.

5.3 Rudi's Cabana
Steven Mannell, 1998

(Left to right) Small scale model study; Framing the cabana; Screens and shadows.
(Opposite page) Local residents look forward to the appearance of these small pavilions every summer.

This was the first of a series of free labs that studied R.M. Schindler's architectural explorations into wood frame construction. Close investigations of the architect's writings and drawings were followed by scale model reconstructions of Schindler's house designs from the 1920s through the 1940s. Only then were students asked to develop their own design for a cabana, using Schindler's building system. The final project was carried out at full scale on the front lawn of the architecture school. Children and adults alike could walk through and linger in the playhouse-like structure with the architectural detailing – a real advertisement for modern design!

How does the "how" of a work of architecture matter, as distinct from the "what"? And what are the architectural potentials unlocked by a study of means and actions? The Schindler frame embodies a deep experience of construction technique within a fluid and nimble spatial imagination. Its technique encompasses not only a "vocabulary" of construction – typical materials and joints – but also a "diction" of construction – characteristic relationships of order and emphasis between material elements and joints.

Steven Mannell

5.4 Schindler Frame and Schindler Surfaces – Rodriguez, How and Kallis House
Steven Mannell, 2002 - 2003

(Left to right) Stud and joist; Rigid frame; Carrying it into position.
(Opposite page) A play of light and shadow on the school lawn.

In subsequent years, Mannell returned to Schindler's work, asking students to revisit various aspects of this complex oeuvre, from framing to cladding.

> *The architectural reenactments presented here study moments of architectural history through performing acts of architecture, undertaking large-scale design-and-build speculation based upon evidence found in action and the transformation of material as well as in text, drawing, and photograph. In analysis, projection, and making, these reenactments propose an understanding of architecture as action and construction as a verb, and seek to engage the nonverbal discourse of the making hand.* Steven Mannell

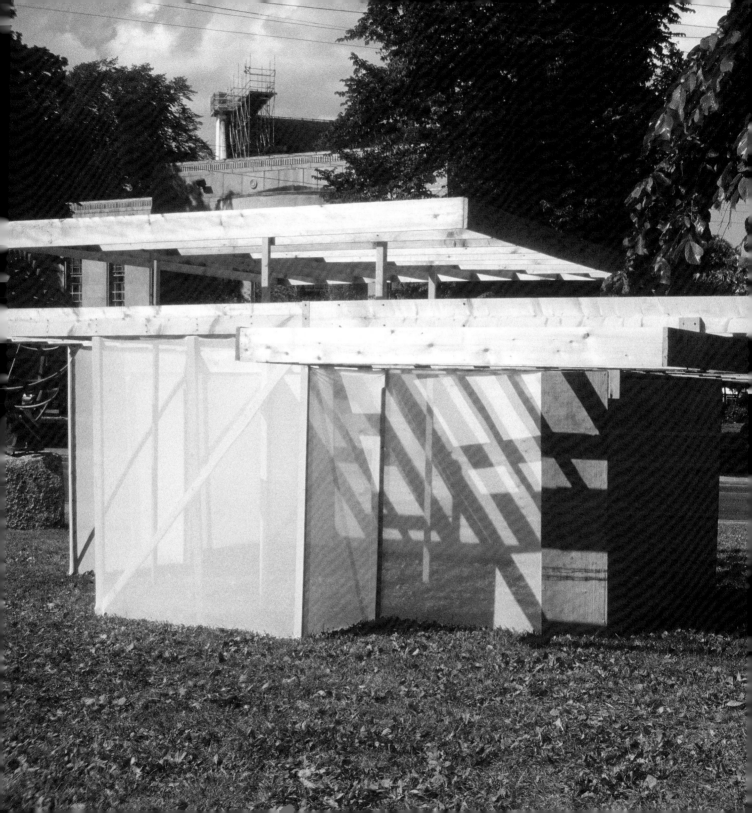

5.5 Prouvé's Propped Type, re-enacted
Steven Mannell, 2000

(Left to right) Study model of the buvette at Evian; An object-lesson for passers-by; Propping up the roof.
(Opposite page) Prouvé's characteristic cantilever frames from inside the pavilion.

This lab studied two of Jean Prouvé's projects from the 1950s that employed a 'propped-type' structure: a school at Villejuif and a buvette at Evian. Students reenacted the erection of this structure to test a central aspect of Prouvé's construction system – the efficient use of human labor on the building site. Prouvé's structural types share certain principles: maximum off-site prefabrication and minimal on-site construction, lightweight components easy for small crews to handle, assembly sequences that allowed each step of the building to serve as scaffolding for the next step, and adjustable joints between components. The propped-type pavilion was realized at a slightly miniaturized scale to make erection of a wooden version easier.

> T- frames and connecting beams were erected and braced by mullions. A mullion assembly opposite was braced at an angle, creating three support points for the roof panels. The large scale model performed as predicted by the small model, although at full scale, with ten people pushing up on the roof edge, the rapid increase in the stiffness and stability of the structure … could literally be felt.   Steven Mannell

5.6   Breuer's American Frame
Steven Mannell, 2004

(Left to right) Study model of the Caesar cottage; Framing and cladding. (Opposite page) Rustic modernism.

In a series of houses built after his move to the United States, Marcel Breuer developed a framing system that was a hybrid between traditional American balloon framing and the platform frame developed in the western states after the Second World War. Using 'two-by' lumber and board sheathing, this composite allowed for significant cantilevers that made the house seem to float above the ground, and reduced foundation work to a minimum. After studying Breuer's Chamberlain cottage of 1940 and his Caesar cottage of a decade later, students designed an original pavilion that incorporated aspects of both.

5.7 Zumthor Chapel

Julian Carnrite, Jerome Cormier, Dan Goltzman, Omar Gandhi, Brian Hanley,
Amelia Hollinghurst, Jason Minard, Kevin Reid, 2003 (Steven Mannell advising)

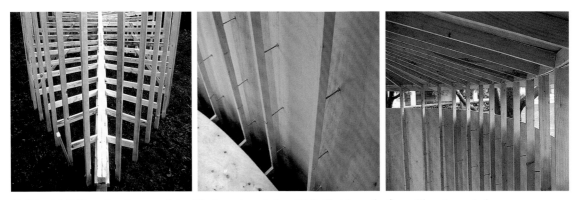

(Left to right) Floor framing complete of the lens-shaped plan; Wall offset from the floor; Clerestory windows.
(Opposite page) A meditative space on the busy street.

This lab studied Peter Zumthor's Chapel of Saint Benedict by building a replica of it at one-third scale. In the process, students discovered a great deal about framing a cylindrical pavilion, from the fan-like arrangements of joists to the expression of roof in frame and surface. Portions of the building were left unclad to expose the logic and beauty of the frame. In building the work at a smaller scale, students had to develop their own details while keeping to the spirit of the original.

5.8 Ghost 1

Brian MacKay-Lyons, 1994

(Left to right) Ghost in the fog; Wrapping the frame in polyurethane; Evening ghost stories around a fire.
(Opposite page) Beacon in the night.

Over the years, MacKay-Lyons has widened his 'ghost' labs to include participants from across North America. Like all of Dalhousie's free labs, it builds architectural knowledge through direct experience, but MacKay-Lyons brings his whole office into the act, as he shares his views on the distinctive landscape, material culture and community of his native province. Each summer, the lab returns to the stone ruins of a nearly 400 year old settlement on the 'Back 40' acres of his estate on the South Shore, and each lab concludes with a evening celebration of feasting and music.

> *Close your eyes and imagine a foggy mid-summer's night. Imagine the glowing, translucent ghosts of archetypal buildings on the ruins of an abandoned village at the edge of the world.*
> Brian MacKay-Lyons

My students began with an amateur archaeological dig, fixing foundation walls and the central hearth of the oldest house in the village. Local elders, carpenters, and artists came and shared their oral history. One hundred cattle joined us on the site. After researching local vernacular building practices, we detailed my design for the Ghost. We built a frame out of logs cut from trees on the hilltop. This frame, which echoed the structure of the old house, was wrapped with a translucent skin, sewn together and rigged up like sails. On the last day, we finished, exhausted, and built a huge fire in the old hearth. As darkness fell the ghost lit up in the fog like a magical lamp. The cattle watched from the shadows as over 100 neighbours and friends were drawn to the ghost; people who had farmed here; a woman who was born in the house; another who as an orphan, had worked as a domestic in the house. Ghost stories followed late into the night, on the dirt floor inside. Brian MacKay-Lyons

5.9 Ghost 2 and 3

Brian Mackay-Lyons, 1995 and 1997

(Left to right) Ghost 2 silhouette at dusk; Ghost 2 showing steps up to platform; Ghost 3 at sunset.
(Opposite page) Working on the frame of Ghost 3 in the fading light.

The second Ghost lab began by hauling down the skeleton of the previous installation. MacKay-Lyons restricted this project to 500 two-by-fours and 150 pounds of common nails, limiting all connections to variations on finger joints. The result was a 100 foot long platform, marked with a stair, well, table and hearth along its length.

Ghost 3 was again a long platform framed in a rhythmic grid of two-by-fours and supported on a series of timber posts set in the ground. Sensitive to the power of wind on this waterfront site, Mackay-Lyons designed a tubular pavilion as a three dimensional lesson in wind shear. Translucent plastic panels served as projection screens for a commemorative tribute to the village matriarch Beulah Oxner on the final evening of the lab.

Appendix

A complete listing of Free Labs, 1991-2006

The Free Labs are listed chronologically, indicating participants, supporting sponsors and community groups. All efforts have been made to ensure accuracy, yet mistakes may remain. Please notify the School of Architecture of any errors, and we will correct them in future printings. Labs indicated with an asterisk are presented in the book.

1991
Birchbark Canoe *
Leader: Richard Kroeker; Participating: Jacob Baker, Marina Cavanaugh, James Davies, Pat McGee, David Nicolay, Fiona Sinclair, Brad Taylor, Lisa Tondino.

Ceramics Workshop
Participating: Marc Cormier, Kim Durno, Carl MacDonald, Michael Machtmes, Stacey MacPherson, Stephen Murray, Marc Paradis, Golsa Soraya.

Fibres Workshop
Participating: Ann McLean, Kelly Hayes, Milana Kosovac, Danny Maher, Janet Pigot, Buddy Rappaport, Alan Scoler.

Identity of Site
Participating: Heidi Bell, Allan Borenstein, Alec Brown, Charles Cox, Darrin Heaton, Kevin Nyhoff, Laura Steele, Mark Tholen.

1994
Bon Portage Island – Acadia University Camp for Biological Research
Leader: Ted Cavanagh; Participating: Aaron Stavert, Diana Carl

Ghost 1*
Leader: Brian MacKay-Lyons; Participating: Matthew Beattie, Nicole Delmage, Carolyn Jeffs, Glenn MacMullin, Zane Murdoch, Jim Pfeffer, Sean Rodrigues, Talbot Sweetapple, Mike Woodland. Photos: p.102 left + right, Nicole Delmage; p.102 centre, Ghost 1 participant; p.103, Nicole Delmage.

Mahone Bay Wayfinder – Wooden Boat Festival
Leader: Christine Macy; Participating: Pierre Bonhomme, Blair Fiset, John Fowke, Brad Garven, Andy Lai, Ephraim Moikebinyane, Fialka Semenuik, Lesley Taylor.

Mi'kmaq Lodges *
Leaders: Richard Kroeker, John Henry Lafford, Albert Marshall and Barry Barnard; Participating: MarMar Cho, David English, Bruce Fraser, Ilona Hay, Jocie Irish, David Lopes, Michael Mulhern, Ferdinand Regier, Patricia West.

Performance Structure – New World Beacons
Leader: Jonathan Hale; Participating: Rob Menchenton

Theatre and Device
Leader: Tony Barlow; Participating: Tom Strickland, Paul Mulak

Remaining B3 class: Dawn Bambrick, Lisette Day, Tim Drennan, Ross Farquhar, Beata Fedak, Terrance Feran, Denise Flemming, Christopher Horsman, Claudine Hounanian, Ken Kam, Rick Kanne, Ben Lau, Samantha Leung, Natalia Lombardi, Kevin Macdonald, Edward Mahzani, Meika McCunn, Joe McGrath, Thad Mermer, Michele Mikic, Stranger Monareng, Ishmael Mosinyi, Sandra Nasrallah, Humphrey Nawa, Ben Nycum, Ken O'Connor, Judy Obersi, Scott Radford, Lorrie Rand, Alexander Ross, Kelly Seminoff, Craig Smith, Isaac Toromba, Chi-Man Trinh, Todd Voshell, Alex Weller.

1995

Ghost 2 – Totemic platform *
Leader: Brian MacKay-Lyons; Participating: Chris Allen, Audrey Archambault, Trevor Davies, Stephanie Forsythe, Rod Gillis, Laura Heald, Alastair Huber, Philip Jefferson, David Jensen, Colleen Lashuk, Alison MacNeil, Christopher Oxner, Michael Rudnicki, Jason Smirnis. Photos: p.104 left + centre, Chris Oxner; p.104 right, Brian MacKay-Lyons; p.105, Mike Farrar.

Landscape Opera *
Leader: Christine Macy; Participating: Delmer Cox, Stephen Inkpen, Shafraaz Kaba, Michelle Lavigne, Aaron Macphee, Jason Mais, Colleen McGrath, Moffat Mothibedi, Robert Porter, Greg Sullivan, Smartex Tambala, Kristin Whiteley, Joe Zareski. Thanks to Angelike Weller and the Manhattan School of Music.

Musical Event + Landscape – Grid Shell and Landscape Performance *
Leaders: Richard Kroeker with John Henry Lafford; Participating: Peter Blakeney, Scott Crichton, Holly Hamilton, Stephen Inkpen. Shafraaz Kaba, Michelle Lavigne, Dave Lewis, Robert MacPhee, Jason Mais, Colleen McGrath, Moffat Mothibedi, Maria Napolitano, Scott Pomeroy, Robert Porter, Robert Strange, Greg Sullivan, Kristin Whiteley, Joe Zareski, Thanks to Angelike Weller and the Manhattan School of Music.

Stage
Leader: Christopher Quek; Participating: Jae-do Chung, Delmer Cox, Bernice Cutler, David Ferron, Douglas Fu, Neema Kulkarni, Joseph Lau, Tracey MacTavish, Edward Mazhani, Marta McDermott, Sandy McKay, Renee Murphy, John Nadarajah, Cassie Noseworthy, Lorrie Rand, Smartex Tambala, Christine Ward, Lenworth Wynter, Derek Zakaib.

Story Arch – Installation for the G7 Summit *
Leader: Christine Macy; Participating: Jae-do Chung, Delmer Cox, Bernice Cutler, David Ferron, Douglas Fu, Neema Kulkarni, Joseph Lau, Tracey MacTavish, Edward Mazhani, Marta McDermott, Renee Murphy, John Nadarajah, Cassie Noseworthy, Lorrie Rand, Smartex Tambala, Christine Ward, Lenworth Wynter, Derek Zakaib, Collaborators: Grade 7 students from Rockingham School. With thanks to the Halifax Port Authority for use of the Pier 21 sheds, and to the Nova Scotia Department of Education and Culture for financial support.

1996

Records of many of the labs held this year have been lost, so individual lab participation cannot be indicated.
The labs were: Building a Fragile Environment – Island of Bon Portage (Ted Cavanagh), Building Between – An Interpretive Construction in the Intertidal Zone (Geoff Holton), Freshwater Creek Restoration (Christine Macy), Reading at the Beach (Tim Savage), Skin of the Earth (Richard Kroeker) and Summer Kitchen (Kim Thompson and Jean D'Aragon).

Students participating were: Rizal Abdulrahman, Amy Alfon, Catherine Allen, Chris Allen, Audrey Archambault, Nurhaya Baniyamin, Joyce Bennett, Robert Billard, Peter Blakeney, Peter Bogaczewicz, Marco Bonaventura, Benjamin Checkwitch, Scott Crichton, Jae-do Chung, Delmer Cox, Bernice Cutler, Trevor Davies, Lisette Day, Carolyn Dion, Benoit Dugas, Beata Fedak, Susan Fitzgerald, Ken Forner, Stephanie Forsythe, Douglas Fu, Christine Giguere, Fernanda Hannah-Suarez, Czeslaw Hawryluk, Laura Heald, Paul Hehir, Caja Hoffmann, Agnes Hor, Alastair Huber, Stephen Inkpen, David Jensen, Darryl Jonas, Shafraaz Kaba, Janet Koshuta, Neema Kulkarni, Suzanne Landry, Shawn LaPointe, Colleen Lashuk, Michelle Lavigne, Joseph Lau, Katherine Laycock, Stéphane LeBlanc, David Lewis, John MacNeil, Tracey MacTavish, Jason Mais, Cindy Marcinyk, Marta McDermott, Scott McFadden, Colleen McGrath, Alison McNeil, Gordon Morrison, Moffat Mothibedi, Tony Mukangura, Paul Mulak, John Nadarajah, Cassie Noseworthy, Vincent Nugroho, Ken O'Connor, Christopher Oxner, Martine Paquin, Jean-David Paré, Scott Pomeroy, Robert Porter, Lorrie Rand, Michael Rudnicki, Michael Salmon, Fialka Semenuik, Jay Smirnis, Alec Smith, Robert Strange, Greg Sullivan, Stefania Sverrisdóttir, Smartex Tambala, Rahim Tejani, Mélanie Thibault, Christine Ward, Christopher Wegner, Alex Weller, Kristen Welton, Marcus Wheeler, Kristin Whiteley, Man Kin Wong, Shyue-Jiun Woon, Thomas Wright, Derek Zakaib, Joe Zareski.

1997

Ghost 3 – Wind Tube *
Leader: Brian MacKay-Lyons; Participating: Maheira Abdel Aziz, Benn Duffell, Michael Farrar, Nicola Grigg, Ron Isaac, Viktoria Mogyoro, Richard Nowlan, Trevor Thimm, Krista Wuerr.

Landings – Beach Wall *
Leader: Niall Savage; Participating: Kelly Chow, Chad Jamieson, Beth Lewis, Kathryn Mitchell, Patricia Piwowar, Wes Wollin, Vicco Yip, Patrick Yue.

Sweat – Portable Collapsible Sweatlodge
Leader: Christine Macy; Participating: Nehal Abdel Aziz, Benjamin Beckwith, Jason Gay, William King, Suzanne Landry, Carrie Thornhill, Ian Wagschal.

Tensile Pattern *
Leader: Sarah Bonnemaison; Participating: Yun Kiong (Albert) Chan, Marc Gaudet, Marla Guay, Andy Moy, Antonio Shin, Darren Newton, Anton Pertschy, Karey Thatcher.

Beaverbank Lattice Shell
Leaders: Richard Kroeker and Steven Mannell, with John Henry Lafford, Laureen van Lierop and Clinton Terry; Participating: Deborah Eaton, Katy Laycock, Anne Marie Jacobsen, Susan Parmley, David Scott, Bruno Weber, Stefan Wong, Jean Yau. With thanks to Dr. Chris Williams from the University of Bath.

1998

Birchtown Pavilions *
Leader: Richard Kroeker; Participating: Curtis Dyck, Emmanuel Gaopotlake, Chad Jamieson, Joo-Hwan Kim, William King, Chung Lee, Parker McIsaac, Kathryn Mitchell, Patricia Piwowar, Jurij Sennecke, Ly Tang. With thanks to the Black Loyalist Heritage Society.

Erratic Net at Peggy's Cove *
Leader: Philip Beesley; Participating: Kelly Chow, Chris Ferguson, Nicola Grigg, Sandra Lee, Beth Lewis, Sunil Sarwal, Thomas Wright, Vicco Yip.

Lightweight Wood Columns
Leader: Christine Macy; Participating: Maheira Abdel Aziz, Nehal Abdel Aziz, Marc Gaudet, Andy Moy, Darren Newton, Susan Parmley, David Scott, Genevieve Sopchuck, Jennifer Uegama; Research assistants: Roger Mullin, Chris Oxner, Martine Paquin. Project funding from the University / Industry Research and Development Partnership Program (InNOVAcorp), in partnership with Filum Ltd.

North End Garden
Leaders: Ted Cavanagh and Judy Obersi; Participating: Carina Cojeen, Melanie Hayne, Ron Isaac, Anne Marie Jacobsen, Tom Kanellopoulos, Phooko Phooko, Trevor Thimm, Carrie Thornhill, Trina Tiller, Ming Feng Tsai, Ian Wagschal.

Rain/ Roof/ Rock
Leader: Peter Henry; Participating: Sarah Bjornson, James Bugden, Roland Chan, Suzanne Doucet, Graham Gavine, Cameron Gillies, Gurinder Grewal, Ania Gudelewicz, Christa MacArthur, Nova Tayona, Patrick Yue.

Rudi's Cabana *
Leader: Steven Mannell; Participating: Benn Duffell, Laura Evans, Michael Farrar, Katy Laycock, Viktoria Mogyoro, Dale Parkes, Brady Peters, Antonio Shin, Aneirin Smith, Karey Thatcher, Melissa White. Financial support provided by the Canadian Wood Council. Project materials generously donated by Barrett Lumber.

Ruskin's Seven Lamps Revisited – on Chocolate Lake
Leader: Tony Barlow; Participating: Amy Alfon, Yun Kiong (Albert) Chan, Catherine McMahon, Cecilia Nin, Leslie Parker, Mpho Tau, Bruno Weber, Natalie Wee, Wes Wollin, Stefan Wong, Krista Wuerr.

Virtues of Wood
Leader: Christopher Quek; Participating: Stephanie Clancy, David Eqbal, Noel Faytone, Rick Fowler, Melanie Hayne, Marisa Huque, Morgan Meier, Richard Nowlan, Rahim Tejani, Andrew Toker, Lazarus Yotamu.

1999
Automatic Topologies
Leader: Patrick Harrop; Participating: Heather Barrington, Heather Bown, Jean-Francois Cyr, Laura Evans, Annelise Johns, Christiane McAlister, Dale Parkes, Sunil Sarwal, Jennifer Ujimoto, Steven Waugh, David Yuen.

Beach Mobile
Leader: Terri Fuglem; Participating: Effie Bouras, Stephanie Clancy, David Eqbal, Terry Kim, Morgan Meier, Ralston Mooring, Tina Smith, Nova Tayona, Cameron Veres.

Building Naturally *
Leader: Kim Thompson; Participating: Ben Beckwith, Hugo Hardy, Melinda Hart, Ryan Hicks, Pat Jost, Monique MacEwan, Ken Matende, Leora Rota, Ken Shaman, Mike Suen, Lynda Ursaki. Special thanks to Rod Malay, Athena and Bill Steen, and Caigeann Thompson.

Community Garden
Leader: Ted Cavanagh; Participating: James Bugden, Courtney Clarke, Emmanuel Gaopotlake, Ahmed Abdel Halim, Wendy James, Joo Hwan Kim, Carol Savoie, Ly Tang, Ming Feng Tsai, Dawn Wagner, Jean Yau.

Découpage
Leader: Janet Koshuta; Participating: Albert Chan, Roland Chan, Michael Farrar, Cameron Gillies, Phooko Phooko, Melissa White.

Mexico City – Three Eras of the *Zocalo* *
Leaders: Sarah Bonnemaison and Christine Macy; Participating: Pauline Alam, Liz Anderson, Noel Faytone, Marisa Huque, Mikko Leppanen, Parker McIsaac, Cecilia Nin Hernandez, Marnie Pardee, Ryan Scarff, Jennifer Uegama. Guests: Prof. Ernesto Alva, Dr. Gabriel Merigo Basurto. Arq. Estafania Chavez de Ortega. With thanks for the generous support of Tere Hannah, and funding from the Canada Council.

Nova Scotia Designer Craft Council Conference Table
Leader: Peter Henry; Participating: Justin Bennett, Martin Christensen, Aaron Costain, Deborah Eaton, Brian Kikstra, David Leung, Christa MacArthur, Marc Mazerolle, Geoff Miller, William Sharpe, Mpho Tau.

Nova Scotia Home for Coloured Children
Leader: Matthew Beattie; Participating: Suzanne Doucet, Curtis Dyck, Melanie Hayne, Sandra Lee, Natalie Wee, Man Kin Wong.

Polyethylene Party
Leader: Ben Checkwitch; Participating: Chris Ferguson, Ania Gudelewicz, Chung Lee, Miyako Panalaks, Leslie Parker, Trina Tiller.

Site - Studio - Site
Leader: Roger Mullin; Participating: Sarah Bjornson, Simon Di Vicenzo, Marla Guay, Aneirin Smith, Vicco Yip, Joe Zingaro.

Virtues of Wood 2
Leader: Christopher Quek; Participating: James Blanchard, Richard Boro, André Boudreau, Keenen Chin, Alan Eisner, Katie Everett, Hady Mousa, Troy Holloway, Stanley Hsu, Daniel Kronby, Matt Taylor.

2000

Beach Bang! A-Go-Go!
Leader: Terri Fuglem; Participating: Tammy Allison, Heather Colwell, Joylyn Marshall, Jared Regier, Ryan Scarff, Celeste Whalen, Roseanne Wong.

Documentation of the Blue Cottage at Huntington Point, NS
Student-led lab with: Pauline Alam, Jennet Bowdridge, Wendy James, Carol Savoie, Lynda Ursaki (Richard Kroeker advising).

Mov-ibles – Atelier/ Loft/ Pavilion *
Leader: Marie-Paule Macdonald; Participating: Richard Boro, David Cameron, Roger Green, Christopher Holmes, Robert Huber, Bernard Mhaladi, Sakgomo Maruping, Lee Miller, Arnold Nasha, Peter Osborne, Wayne Pai, David Vera, Brian Warford, David Yuen. Photos: Marie-Paule Macdonald.

114

Prouvé's Propped-type Pavilion, Re-enacted *
Leader: Steven Mannell; Participating: Heather Bown, Keenen Chin, Aaron Costain, Stanley Hsu, Brian Kikstra, Daniel Kronby, David Leung, Geoffrey Miller, Tina Smith, Michael Suen. Material and financial support from the Nova Scotia College of Art and Design, Barrett Lumber, and Metal Supermarket.

Sauna at Lake Magaguadavic, NB
Student-led lab with: Jill Hynes, Orianne Johnson, David Kitazaki, Tara Murray (Terri Fuglem advising).

Studies of London
Leader: Philip MacAleer; Participating: Elizabeth Anderson, Cory Dobbin, Katie Everett, Patrick Jost, Mikko Leppanen, Daniel Lothstein, Monique MacEwan, Tyler Sharp, Adriana Shum, Jennifer Ujimoto.

Tree to Wood
Leader: Richard Kroeker; Participating: Christopher Bowes, James Bugden, Roland Chan, Jon Gottlieb, Gurinder Grewal, Hugo Hardy, Troy Holloway, Annelise Johns, Diana Liu, Catherine McMahon, Clausen Morapedi, Marnie Pardee, Marina Ramirez, Sunil Sarwal.

Other student-led free labs by: Christopher Beamer, Nolan Bentley, Majida Boga, Andre Boudreau, Effie Bouras, Lee Cameron, Winston Chong, Deanna Clarke, Courtney Clarke, Daniel Cohlmeyer, Sandra Cook, Ben Cotter, Anna Craig, Marc Mazerolle, Caroline Miller, Troy Scott, Ken Shaman, Scott Silverberg, Vincent Siu, Vjekica Sucic, Matthew Taylor, Joy Tayona, Cameron Veres, Dawn Wagner, Gary Watson, Steven Waugh, Vicco Yip.

2001

There were no free labs in 2001, however, two "research labs" were offered as electives.

Bricks
Leaders: Steven Mannell with Basil Kilgar. Participating: Roger Green, Robert Huber, Christiane McAlister, and Peter Osborne. With thanks to Bert Frizzell and Terry McDow of Shaw Brick for financial and material support.

West Wing – Eskasoni Studio and Conference Room *
Leader: Richard Kroeker; Client: Murdena Marshall; Participating: Hady Mousa, Ben Cotter, Wesley Gowing, Kevin Loewen, Bernard Mhaladi, Paul Wu.

2002

Birchtown Benches *
Leader: Christine Macy; Participating: Tetsushi Aoki, Youki Cropas, Rebekka Hammer, Michelle McDonough, Raelyn Moore, Lefoko Simako, Ryan Thorne. With thanks to Ken Brown and the Black Loyalist Heritage Society.

Cocoon
Leader: Sarah Bonnemaison; Participating: Jolene Anderson, Amanda Doiron, Marc Guillemette, Wai Lui, Cian McGarvey, Nancy Nashed, Yirenkyi'wa Ohene-Fianko, Juliet Pitts, Stuart Rostant, Kutobe Tshabang, Shonda Wheaton.

An Architectural Folly at the TUNS gazebo
Leader: Dimitri Procos; Participating: Raymonde Arsenault, Julian Carnrite, Jerome Cormier, J.R. Feeney, Dale Flanders, Jesse Hindle, Henry Howard, Douglas Mayr, Rebecca Mifflin, Mpho Mogasha, Terry Tremayne, Kenrad Wilchcombe,

From Drawing to Building *
Leader: Anthony Viscardi; Participating: Craig Brimley, Grace Chan, Erik Cunnington, J.P. Felix, Brian Hanley, Nick Herder, Amelia Hollingshurst, Stephanie Hui, Jason Minard, Nelson Mothibakgomo, Robert Osbourne, Kevin Reid, Evan Spence, Natasha van den Berg, Roseanne Wong.

Gully Bridge, PEI*
Leader: Roger Mullin; Participating: Jeremy Bryant, Kelli Davis, Beth Denny, Melissa Freeman, Persis Lam, Rachel Langille, Chris Lee, Marc MacCaull, Jeff Skinner.

Ripped Gridded Ribbon – Grid Shell *
Leader: Peter Sassenroth; Participating: Shamim Alaei, David Cameron, Ivan Chu, Alex Pigott, Dean Poffenroth, Morgan Power, Leago Sebina, Anthony Sekgweng, Nadine Williams, Eli Wolpin.

Schindler Frame – Rodriquez House *
Leader: Steven Mannell; Participating: Craig Abercrombie, Jeremy Bryant, Olly Chibua, Johnny Chimienti, Marwa El-Kady, Greg Fry, Omar Gandhi, Elena Garcia, Jay Gillman, Emily Kearns, John Mosimenyane, Scott MacNeill, Marina Ramirez, Colin Turner, Stephen Terauds. With thanks to Piercey's Building Supplies for donation of building materials.

Strawbale Construction
Student-led lab with: Charlotte Dunfield, Sheena Gilman; Veronica Madonna, Tero Malcolm, Caroline Miller, Jared Regier (Kim Thompson advising). Special thanks to Jeff Achenbach and Rod Malay.

West Wing – Eskasoni Studio 2 – cladding *
Leader: Richard Kroeker; Client: Murdena Marshall; Participating: Mark Anson, Danielle Churchill, Craig Cowan, Sophia Dobrev, Daniel Goltzman, Andree Lalonde, Alden Neufeld, Martin Patriquin, Christine Thornton, Michelle Yeung, Emmy Young, Chris Woodford, Cheryle Wong.

Self-directed: Heather Barrington, Stephanie Davidson, Mitz Delisle, Johneen Manning, Arnold Nasha, Patricia Russell.

2003

Architecture in Motion 1 – *Traces* at the Basilica Industria in Hudson, New York *
Leaders: Sarah Bonnemaison and Christine Macy; Participating: Grace Chan, Robert Des Rosiers, Colin Gash, Anna Kramer, WeiWei Lin, Georgina Lyons, Nancy Nashed, Erica Pecoskie, Nina Rubenstein, Lefoko Simako, Natasha Somborac, Kutobe Tshabang, Keith Tufts, Michelle Yeung; Choreographers: Sondra Loring and Jill-Ann Schwartz; Collaborators: Isa Coffey, Tatiana Margitic, Anne Mulvaney, Takemi Kitamura. Financial support provided by the New York State DanceForce, Artist in Action Series.

Camera Obscura *
Leader: Ken Kam; Participating: Vivian Au, Patrick Cheung, Andrée Lalonde, Jenn Lau, Kevin Lee, Johneen Manning, Raelyn Moore, Patrick Rizk, Christine Thornton, Cara Tretiak.

Finding Form – Cylindrical Shell *
Leader: Roger Mullin; Participating: Simon Ellison, Raphael Gogniat, Daniel Goltzman, Kevin Harrison, Stephanie Lam, Zihuan Lin, Alanna Molloy, Judah Mulalu, Ron Pettipas, Jessica Ryan, Trina Whitehurst, Barry Wong.

Sheet Metal
Leader: Dimitri Procos; Participating: Melanie Abbott, Craig Abercrombie, Craig Cowan, Frank Galoni, Jay Gillman, Henry Howard, Elizabeth Jong, Robert Osbourne, Evan Spence, Aaron Taylor, Kenrad Wilchcombe.

Schindler Surfaces – How and Kallis Houses *
Leader: Steven Mannell; Participating: Michael Colpitts, Lian Cronje, Youki Cropas, Marc Guillemette, Rebekka Hammer, Rory Heath, Jordan Ludington, Marc MacCaull, Cian McGarvey, Allegra Snyder, Jennifer Wilson, Emmy Young. With thanks to Judith Sheine for her participation in the inaugural seminar and her assistance with documentary materials, and to Piercey's Building Supplies for donation of materials.

Spine of the Dragon – Shambhala Outdoor Classroom *
Leader: Kim Thompson; Participating: Tetsushi Aoki, Olly Chibua, Mitz Delisle, Catherine Desjardins, Amanda Doiron, Kevin Fisher, Albert Lee, Stuart Rostant, Rachel Slipp-Langille, Sean Serino, Colin Turner, Shonda Wheaton, Jennifer Young, Marcela Zurita. Donations of building material were generously provided by Brian Lewis Excavating. Thanks to Steve Mustain, Kevin Cormish, Deborah Ross, and students and parents from the Shambhala School.

Fixing the Light *
Leader: Kourosh Mahvash; Participating: Danielle Churchill, Sophia Dobrev, J.P. Felix, Greg Fry, Alex Kravec, Janet Loebach, Farhad Mawani, Michelle McDonough, Ching-Te Earl Peng, Tim Schmitt, Jeff Skinner, Sandra Thomson. Photos: p.78 left, Ken Kam; p.78 centre, Greg Fry; p.78 right, J.P. Felix; p.79, Ken Kam.

West Wing – Eskasoni Studio 3 – interior *
Leader: Richard Kroeker; Client: Murdena Marshall; Participating: Derek Brennan, Maginnis Cocivera, Erik Cunnington, Tyler Dixon, Kelly Dodman, Patrick Jardine, Jennifer Holmes, Mark Lee, Nuria Montblanch, Geoff Moote, Gabriel Prost, Yiming Wang.

Zumthor's St. Benedict Chapel *
Student-led lab with: Julian Carnite, Jerome Cormier, Omar Gandhi, Brian Hanley, Amelia Hollingshurst, Kevin Reid. (Steven Mannell advising). Photos: p.101, Omar Gandhi. With thanks to Piercey's Building Supplies for donation of materials and Dale Arsenault for lending us an air nailer.

2004

Architecture in Motion 2 – *Shadows* at the Ross Creek Centre for the Arts, NS *
Leaders: Sarah Bonnemaison, Christine Macy and Kourosh Mahvash; Participating: Robert Des Rosiers, Kristin James, Anna Kramer, Sam Laffin, Dawn Lang, Alanna Molloy, Robert McGill, Christine Ng, Alana Paon, Simon Pirquet, Rubeena Saran, Sarah Schaefer, Anna Silverstein, Corinne Yarmuch; Research collaborators: Sondra Loring, Ariella Pahlke, Jill-Ann Schwartz; Dancers: Anne Mulvaney, Maria Osende; Additional lighting: Ken Schwartz. Project funding from Social Sciences and Humanities Research Council, with additional support from the Ross Creek Centre for the Arts.

Birchtown Interpretive Trail and Pit House *
Leader: Christine Macy; Participating: Laura Feddersen, Vincent Mokomele, Kelly Smith, Jordan Winters, Kent Yiu. With thanks to David Carter of the Nova Scotia Museum, and the Black Loyalist Heritage Society.

88 Constellations for Wittgenstein
Leaders: David Clark and Brian Lilley; Participating: Vivian Au, Albert Cheng, Maginnis Cocivera, Yirenkyiwa Ohene-Fianko, Jennifer Holmes, WeiWei Lin, Amy Newborn, David Nightingale, Dominic Paiva, Nikala Reashor.

Crystal Crescent Boardwalk *
Leader: Catherine Venart; Participating: Julien Boudreau, Chris Crawford, Marwa El-Kady, Lise Fournier, Rayleen Hill, Michelle Johnson, Gordon Karau, Dawn Lang, Chris Lee, Ryan Mitchell, Juliet Pitts, Stephen Terauds.

Funhouses
Leaders: Ilona Hay and Claire Weldon; Participating: Mihai Adam, Douglas Choo, Jenny Chow, Michael Colpitts, Raphael Gogniat, Hardy Huang, Gordon Karau, Jordan Ludington, Stephen Van der Meer.

One, Two or Three Minute Film
Leader: Ken Kam; Participating: Melanie Abbott, Michelle Bryck, Ardis Cheng, Alex Kravec, Jenn Lau, Josh Nowlan, Ching-Te Earl Peng, Athena Photinopoulos, Aaron Taylor, Gary Thai, Erica Wang. Thanks to David Middleton.

Breuer's American Frame *
Leader: Steven Mannell; Participating: Jeff Atchison, Laura Alvey, Kirsty Bruce, Michael Cogan, Son Thanh Diep, Noah Epstein, Mark Harrington, Christy Hillman, Sony Rai, Deborah Williams.With thanks to Kent Building Supplies for discounted building materials.

Sono InterVENTion
Leader: Drew Klassen; Participating: Erin Hunt, Persis Lam, Kevin Lee, Iliah Lorenz-Luca, Farhad Mawani, James McCallan, Jessica Ryan, Anna Silverstein, Cara Tretiak, Kirk Weppler.

Saint Joseph's Daycare Playground *
Leader: Kim Thompson; Participating: Jane Abbott, Aimee Drmic, Janna Marie Graham, Marc Guillemette, Rayleen Hill, Jonathan Mandville, Zack Pozebanchuk, Natasha Somborac, Allegra Snyder, Jen Young. Donations of building material were generously provided by the Portland Cement Association, Canadian Tire, and Shaw Brick. Thanks to Lenora Downey, Tomas Brask, and other staff and students from St. Joseph's Quinpool Daycare.

Théâtre Petit Cercle – Chéticamp, Cape Breton Island *
Leaders: Ted Cavanagh, Richard Kroeker, Roger Mullin and Alden Neufeld; Participating: Velma Anelo, Derek Brennan, Kingman Brewster, Catherine Desjardins, Colin Gash, Lynden Giles, Alexander Graf, Deana Hall, Kagiso Jobe, Keemenao Kekobilwe, Mark Lee, Etienne Lemay, Zihuan Lin, Colin Merriam, Benno Rottlaender, Weronika Rybacka, Michelle Sparks, Michael Thicke, Christine Thornton, Robert Toth, Keith Tufts, Mareike Wellers, Vincent Yen. Support from The Arts Council of Chéticamp, and the Chéticamp Co-op.

Wooden Monkey – Outdoor furniture *
Student-led lab with: Tyler Dixon, Kelly Dodman, Gabe Prost, Sony Rai, Yiming Wang, Barry Wong (Steven Mannell advising).

2005

Ambient Material – Recycling Depot in Sackville, NS *
Leader: Richard Kroeker; Participating: Jonathan Carmichael, Son Thanh Diep, Lynden Giles, Dion Lassu, Iliah Lorenz-Luca, Robert McGill, Jesse Ratcliffe, Nikala Reashor, Rubeena Saran, Anna Silverstein, Sara Stratton, Jordan Winters.

Architecture in Motion 3 – *Gestures* at the Maritime Museum, Halifax *
Leaders: Sarah Bonnemaison and Christine Macy; Participating: Richard Blouin, Michael Cogan, Stephanie da Silva, Emma Fitzgerald, Jacob JeBailey, Kelvin Nyathi, Alicia Yip, Velma Anelo, Kirsty Bruce, Sam Laffin, Laura Mathison, Simon Pirquet, Timothy Schmitt, Kelly Smith, Robert Toth, Kirk Weppler; Research collaborators: Ariella Pahlke, Maria Osende; Research assistants: Joel Dauncey, Marwa El-Kady, Greg Fry. Project funding from Social Sciences and Humanities Research Council, with additional support from the Digital Animation Department of the Nova Scotia Community College in Truro, and the Maritime Museum of the Atlantic. Special thanks to John Hennigar Shuh, Eamonn Doorley, and Mark Scott of the Maritime Museum of the Atlantic; Debbie Smith of the Nova Scotia Community College in Truro; and the Textiles Department of NSCAD U.

Cinecitta
Leader: Andrew King; Participating: Kate Busby, Eric Cheung, Jenny Chow, François Descoteaux, Noah Epstein, Hardy Huang, William MacIvor, Jason Mrdeza, Aaron Outhwaite, Andrea Saldanha, Michael Thicke, Vincent Yen.

Competition
Student-led lab: Laura Alvey, Kelly Dodman, Kristin James, Marcin Sztaba (Catherine Venart advising).

Exit 13A*
Student-led lab with: Simon Ellison, Kevin Harrison, Michelle Johnson, Georgina Lyons, Ryan Mitchell, Geoff Moote, Matt Seegmiller. (Catherine Venart advising).

Flexible Walls – Studio Partitions
Leader: Samantha Rodriguez Machado; Participating: Esha Das, Mark Genest, Isidore Jatta, Rohey Jobe, Setlhomo Xeti Matebekwane, Vincent Mokomele, Sandra Thomson, Cristian Torcat, Gregory Wilson.

Greenhouse *
Leader: Ilona Hay; Participating: Jeffrey Atchison, David Cromp, Catherine MacQuarrie, Refilwe Mompe, Ronald Pettipas, Elizabeth Powell, Elizabeth Sinanan, Erica Wang, Cindy Wood, Corinne Yarmuch. Photos by David Cromp.

In Search of the Missing Church at Grand Pré – an archaeological dig
Leader: Ken Kam; Participating: Albert Cheng, Douglas Choo, Matthew Gise, Deana Hall, Kagiso Jobe, Colin Merriam, Joshua Nowlan, Sarah Schaefer. Thanks to Jonathan Fowler and Rob Ferguson.

Labyrinth *
Leaders: Tim Collett and Patricia West; Participating: Diane Abrera, Kingman Brewster, Jaclyne Clarke, Asher deGroot, Frank Galoni, Ben Gaum, Joshua Lunn, Jenny Mecksavanh, Barbra Moss, Michael Santilli, Andrea Scott, Bradley Thiessen, Dustin Valen, Mandy Wong.

Playful Walls*
Leader: Kim Thompson; Participating: Thea Campbell, Laura Feddersen, David Gallaugher, Ace Kekobilwe, Waterson Lam, Helen Othogile, Melani Pigat, Kate Vanderwater.

Portraits
Student-led lab: Ardis Cheng, James McCallan, Athena Photinopoulos, Michelle Sparks (Ken Kam advising).

Raftwerk – Buoy Line Installation *
Leader: Roger Mullin; Participating: Mihai Adam, Morgan Carter, Robert Downey, Lise Fournier, Erin Hunt, Jonathan Mandville, James Rossa O'Hare, Erica Pecoskie, Annie Pelletier, Jennifer Wilson, Sarah Zollinger, Paul Zylstra. Special thanks to Halifax Port Authority, CN Rail, and McGraw's Marine for permission to use the site.

Restaurant
Student-led lab: Mark Harrington, Christy Hillman, Deborah Williams (Austin Parsons advising).

2006

Architects of Illusion – Perceptions of Deceptions *
Leaders: Eric and Leslie Van Duzer; Participating: Ryan Alward, Colin Carrigan, Jeremiah Deutscher, Shane Gee, Zayyad Mahmoud, Grace Park, Jali Saha, Chen Sheng. Photos: Ken Kam.

Chéticamp Sleeping Cabins *
Leaders: Ted Cavanagh, Roger Mullin and Peter Sassenroth; Participating: Eric Baczuk, David Bourque, Sarah Carlisle, Paul Chafe, Behsheed Darvish, Susan Flynn, Mareko Gaoboe, Eleanor Hopkins, Daniel Korver, Kistro Kelaotswe, Mason Lampard, City Mafa, James Merlevede, Goabaone Ntshontsi, Emilio Williams Portal, Danielle Pottier, Keolopile Rabatsheko, Sony Mark Sin, Sara Theuerkauf. Financial support for the project was provided from the Social Sciences and Humanities Research Council and the Canada Wood Council.

Hot Spot *
Leader: Anke Wollbrink; Participating: Shane Andrews, Claire Belanger, Paul Davies, Nicholas Fudge, Alexandra Gaudreau, Leah Gillis, Teron McConnell Gordon, Blaine Lepp, Matt Malone, Jay Meyer, Robyn Robertson, Matt Rosenberg. Photos by Meinhard Pfanner.

Lightsail *
Leader: Tim Gray; Participating: Lina Ali, Kirsten Bremer, Andrew Cranford, Guy Fimmers, April Hiebert, Luc Johnston, Lauren Macaulay, Michelle Poon, Adam Read, Lauren Staples. Guests / consultants: Geoff Holton, Mark Rumreich. With thanks to Southwest Properties for use of the site, and the Faculty of Engineering at Dalhousie University for use of the machine shop. Photos : p.68 left, Laren Staples; p.68 centre, Guy Fimmers; p.68 right, April Hiebert; p.69 Luc Johnston.

Salvation Army Urban Garden *
Leader: Susan Molesky; Participating: Corrado Agnello, Logan Amos, Adetokunbo Bodunrin, Alexandra Bolen, Kristin Chrzanowski, Melissa Clarke, Tony DiNardo, Mike Eady, Joe Lambert, Christina Persaud, Kristal Stevenot, Victoria Yong-Hing. Financial support for the project was provided by the Kitz Fund of the Faculty of Architecture and Planning. With thanks to the following companies for donation of equipment and materials: Allstar Rebar, Conrad Bros. Sand and Gravel, Dartmouth Ready Mix, Lafarge Cement, MacFarlands Tools and Equipment, Ocean Contractors Limited, Pierceys, Russel Metals, and Shaw Brick; and to the Halifax Regional Water Commission and Halifax Regional Municipality for support. With special thanks to Kim Conrad and Gordon Dickie.

A special thanks to Dale Arsenault and Steve Sekerak, for many years of supporting students in their design-build constructions, in the school's wood shop.

Concrete-wood joint designed by Sam Laffin, Gestures 2005.